Guidelines for the Professional Conduct of the Clergy

Guidelines for the Professional Conduct of the Clergy

CHURCH HOUSE
PUBLISHING

Church House Publishing
Church House
Great Smith Street
London
SW1P 3NZ

ISBN 0 7151 1005 5

Published 2003 by Church House
Publishing for the Convocations
of Canterbury and York

contents

Foreword by the Archbishops of Canterbury and York

By its very nature, pastoral ministry involves great trust. In dealing with the vulnerable and the weak, ministers need the trust both of those to whom they minister and the Church whose ministry it is. In setting out these guidelines for the clergy, the Church hopes to establish the best possible practice amongst all who minister in this calling, which is both theirs and ours.

Following the call and pattern of our Lord, there will always be risk in such a ministry. This cannot be avoided and there are occasions when the clergy must take risks. Yet unwarranted risk must be minimized. We hope that the clergy will welcome these guidelines, both as an aid to improving good practice and also as a warning of potential pitfalls.

Underlying all pastoral ministry must be a life of prayer, both in public and in private. The close walk with God that flows from this devotional life is indispensable for the professional conduct of the clergy.

Pastoral ministry is demanding. The guidelines will not make this ministry any less demanding, but they will help the clergy in using their time and talents wisely and efficiently and to the best advantage of those for whom they care.

The guidelines should improve our practice, our praying and our caring. They need to be kept readily available for reference. We hope that they will be re-read at regular intervals, at least, and appropriately at the renewal of ordination vows or on some other important or significant anniversary. We commend them to the clergy of our two Provinces.

Rowan Cantuar:
David Ebor:
October 2003

Foreword by the Archbishops of Canterbury and York

preface
by the Chairman of the Working Group

This report places before the clergy, bishops, priests and deacons, and the whole Church, guidelines for the professional conduct of all those called to ordained ministry. These are offered by clergy to clergy, but they have significance for the laity to whom the clergy minister and with whom they share the challenge of mission. The Guidelines are not a legal code, but a beginning of an ongoing conversation in which ministers and those to whom they minister need to engage.

The working party received much advice. Some believed the work to be unnecessary. God calls to ministry and the minister should need no other guidelines than the leading of the Holy Spirit. Some seemed to expect the production of detailed regulations running to many volumes covering every aspect of pastoral life. The group, whose report is unanimous, was at one in resisting such temptations and in our conviction that the Guidelines should find their origin in the liturgy of ordination. It is the ordinal which clothes with detail the giving of authority to the minister to be a deacon, priest or bishop in the Church of God. This is where we begin, and the place we revisit to renew our vows and to review our exercise of the authority given to us in the name of Christ.

We have sought to affirm good practice, but to avoid too much detail. We have assumed that the clergy do not need these Guidelines to repeat what they find required of them in Canon Law and we remind ourselves and our fellow ministers of what the law of the Church requires.

At the heart of ministry is risk. Faced with a pastoral situation the minister has to take immediate decisions about what to say and do. These Guidelines are offered to clergy and those who train them as they reflect on what Michael Ramsey called 'the burden of the pastoral office'. We are most grateful to Francis Bridger for his Theological Reflection appended to the Guidelines, which helpfully provide a personal and contemporary perspective.

Guidelines are by their nature not commandments set in stone. It will be for others to keep them under review and as necessary to amend them. Perceptions and demands change and the Guidelines will need to respond to change while holding fast to the basic principles which underlie them.

It has been a privilege to be asked by the Convocations to chair this group and to work with such experienced and talented colleagues. We pray that our work will be of service to all who minister.

Hugh Wilcox
June 2003

Background Note

In February 2000, the Lower Houses of the Convocations of Canterbury and York carried the motion: 'That this House approves the proposal of the Standing Committee of the House of Clergy that a Joint Committee of the two Lower Houses be set up to prepare a Code of Professional Conduct.'

The Joint Committee consisted of the following: Canon Hugh Wilcox (St Albans), Chairman; Canon Frank Dexter (Newcastle); Prebendary Kay Garlick (Hereford); Canon Peter Hill (Southwell); the Revd David Houlding (London) and Canon John Stanley (Liverpool). For the revision process the Rt Revd John Packer (Bishop of Ripon & Leeds) and Mrs Mary Johnston (London) joined the Committee. The Synodical Secretary (Canon Michael Hodge) and the Synodal Secretary (the Venerable David Jenkins) acted as Secretaries to the Joint Committee.

Legal advice was accepted that it would be preferable if the word 'Guidelines' was used rather than 'Code'. A draft document was published in February 2002 and distributed widely. Over 100 responses were received. Both Convocations debated the draft.

Canon Francis Bridger (Principal of Trinity College, Bristol) wrote a 'Theological Reflection' that has been warmly appreciated both by the Working Group and also by those who read it in the draft document. Mrs Diana Webster (Europe) cast an eagle eye over our work, searching for textual infelicities.

The Joint Committee recognizes that what they offer is not, and cannot be, the last word on the subject. It will be for the Standing Committee of the Convocation of Canterbury and the Assessors of the Convocation of York to decide on how to keep the subject under review and to bring forward amendments as necessary from time to time.

guidelines for the professional conduct of the clergy

The primary aims of the Guidelines are:

- to ensure the welfare and the protection of individuals and groups with whom the clergy work;
- to ensure the welfare and the protection of the clergy and of their families;
- to encourage the clergy to aspire to the highest possible standard of conduct;
- to provide safe and effective boundaries for clerical ministry;
- to encourage personal and corporate ministerial development.

1 They must set the Good Shepherd always before them as the pattern of their calling

1.1 The clergy are entrusted with the privilege and responsibility of being servants and leaders in the ministry of the Church. As pastors, spiritual guides and representatives of the Christian faith, they are in a position of trust in their relationships with those for whom they have pastoral care. These Guidelines seek to provide an agreed framework of professional conduct for all clergy as both an encouragement and an affirmation of good practice.

1.2 The clergy will often find themselves in the powerful position of meeting people at the limits of their vulnerability. The Guidelines seek to safeguard and reassure such people, so engendering trust, without which ministry cannot take place.

1.3 All personal and professional conduct is bounded by law and legal sanction. For the clergy, who at ordination swear the Oaths of Obedience and make the Declaration of Assent, this will include ecclesiastical and canon law. However, response to a vocation to serve as an ordained minister signifies the voluntary undertaking of obligations of sacrificial self-discipline above and beyond the requirements of secular and ecclesiastical law. The Ordinal outlines these undertakings and thus guides conduct, so it is the Ordinal that has been used to provide the inspiration and the framework for these Guidelines.

2 Caring for the poor, the needy, the sick, and all who are in trouble

2.1 Caring for one another is the responsibility of the whole Church and is an extension of the justice and love of the Incarnate God disclosed in Jesus Christ. Compassion is essential to pastoral care. The clergy should enable other members of the worshipping community to share in this pastoral care.

2.2 The clergy have a particular responsibility to minister sensitively and effectively to the sick, the dying and the bereaved.

2.3 In their ministry, pastoral care and working relationships, the clergy must endeavour to offer equal respect and opportunity to all.

2.4 The clergy minister through their own broken humanity, being aware of their own need to receive ministry.

2.5 The clergy should discern and make clear their own limitations of time, competence and skill. At times they will need to seek support, help and appropriate training.

2.6 The difference between pastoral care and formal counselling is always to be recognized.

2.7 The clergy should be aware of the help available from accredited agencies so that it can be commended where appropriate.

2.8 There is risk in all pastoral work. The place of the meeting, the arrangement of furniture and lighting, and the dress of the minister are important considerations in pastoral care. The appropriateness of visiting and being visited alone, especially at night, needs to be assessed with care. The clergy should recognize the importance of knowing themselves and their own emotional needs.

2.9 It is essential in pastoral care to acknowledge appropriate physical, sexual, emotional and psychological boundaries. Inappropriate touching or gestures of affection are to be avoided.

2.10 The clergy should be aware of the dangers of dependency in pastoral relationships. Manipulation, competitiveness or collusion on either side of the pastoral encounter should be avoided. Self-awareness should be part of the relationship.

2.11 The clergy should be aware of the potential for abusing their privileged relationships.

2.12 When help or advice is being sought, any note-taking should be mutually agreed and is subject to data protection legislation.

2.13 Every ordained person should have appropriate training in child protection. National and diocesan guidelines and requirements must be known and observed.

3 In the name of the Lord we bid you remember the greatness of the trust now to be committed to your charge

You cannot bear the weight of this ministry in your own strength, but only by the grace and power of God

3.1 Pastoral care will seek to bring about Christ-like wholeness, both personal and corporate. The development of trust is of primary importance for honest relationships within ministry.

3.2 The clergy are placed in a position of power over others, in pastoral relationships, with lay colleagues, and sometimes with other clergy. This power needs to be used to sustain others and harness their strengths, and not to bully, manipulate or denigrate.

3.3 In pastoral and caring relationships the clergy should be open to God and to the needs of the other person. It is important for clergy to be sensitive to the situations in which they are placed, especially with regard to the pastoral care of children, young people and vulnerable adults.

3.4 The clergy should be aware that those for whom they care may be distressed and vulnerable. The power conferred on a minister in such situations should be acknowledged, used positively, and never abused.

3.5 It is always wrong to exploit or manipulate. Improper questioning or physical contact (see 2.9) can be emotionally or sexually abusive.

3.6 Spiritual authority must be exercised with gentleness and sensitivity, and the minister should be aware of the possibility of spiritual abuse.

3.7   Pastoral care should never seek to remove the autonomy given to the individual. In pastoral situations the other party should be allowed the freedom to make decisions that may be mistaken.

3.8   In leadership, teaching, preaching and presiding at worship, the clergy should resist all temptation to exercise power inappropriately.

3.9   The clergy should thankfully acknowledge their own God-given sexuality. They should be aware of the danger of seeking sexual advantage, emotionally or physically, in the exercise of their ministry.

3.10   In their personal life the clergy should set an example of integrity in relationships and faithfulness in marriage.

3.11   A person seeking pastoral guidance and counsel from the clergy has the right to expect that the clergy person concerned will not pass on to a third party confidential information so obtained, without their consent or other lawful authority.

3.12   Unless otherwise agreed, the clergy are accordingly not at liberty to share confidential information with their spouses, family or friends.

3.13   The content and process of a pastoral relationship may need to be shared with certain other people, such as a supervisor or supervisory group, consultant or other involved colleagues. Such sharing needs to be carefully restricted so that it does not involve any breach of confidence. Should it be desirable to discuss the relationship in such a way as to involve a breach of confidentiality, the consent of the person seeking pastoral guidance must first be obtained.

3.14   The clergy should be aware of the circumstances in which confidential information can or should be disclosed to third parties, particularly where the safety of children is concerned. In these circumstances, the clergy should refer to the guidance in the national and diocesan child protection policies. Children or vulnerable adults who disclose evidence of significant harm will need to know that their concerns will be taken seriously and referred to the appropriate statutory agency (usually Social Services) so that a proper investigation can take place and practical help be obtained. In such cases the welfare of the child or vulnerable adult should be regarded as of paramount importance. If contemplating such a disclosure, however, the clergy should seek appropriate legal and other specialist advice. Special considerations apply where information is disclosed in the context of formal confession (see paragraphs 7.2 and 7.3).

3.15 It is important to safeguard the right of parishioners to share personal information with one minister and not another. In a team situation, it may be advisable to create a policy to avoid the danger to ministers within a team of being manipulated and divided by the sharing of personal information with one and not another. Assistant clergy in training posts should make it clear that information given to them will normally be shared with their training incumbent.

3.16 Any information about a living individual, whether held on computer or in a paper-based filing system, will be governed by the Data Protection Act 1998. The clergy should therefore familiarize themselves with the requirements of that legislation and act in accordance with them, seeking advice from their diocesan data protection officer when necessary. Compliance with the legislation may require, amongst other things, formal notification to the Information Commissioner where information about a living individual is held on computer.

3.17 Those compiling records should be prepared to be accountable for their content.

4 Search out the careless and the indifferent

You are to be messengers, watchmen, and stewards of the Lord ... which faith the Church is called upon to proclaim afresh in each generation

4.1 Mission is a primary clerical calling. It belongs to the whole church and the clergy have a leading share of responsibility in its promotion.

4.2 The clergy have the privilege of leading their congregations in proclaiming afresh the Good News of Jesus Christ and promoting mission, including evangelism.

4.3 All schools, along with other institutions within a parish, may provide opportunities for mission and ministry, and a church school is a particular responsibility for the clergy. The clergy should seek to enhance opportunities for themselves and appropriately gifted and trained laity to contribute to the worship, religious education, pastoral care and governance in the church school.

4.4 The clergy should ensure that well-led and accessible courses and discussion groups on all aspects of the Christian faith are available at regular intervals to parishioners seeking to explore, deepen or renew their faith.

4.5 Suitable preparation for Baptism, Confirmation and Marriage is a primary responsibility for the clergy.

4.6 The clergy should recognize, affirm and encourage the ministry and witness of lay people in their workplaces and communities.

5 Teach ... admonish ... feed ... provide for the Lord's family

5.1 Continued theological learning is an essential discipline for preaching and teaching, as well as for personal growth.

5.2 The clergy should set aside time for continuing ministerial education, including the consideration of contemporary issues and theological developments, so that their faith engages with the perceptions and concerns of this generation.

5.3 Keeping abreast of a whole variety of communicating skills is crucial to the effective and ongoing proclamation of the gospel.

5.4 Part of the clerical vocation in both preaching and teaching is a prayerful openness to being prophetic and challenging as well as encouraging and illuminating.

5.5 Great care should be taken that illustrative material from personal experience does not involve any breach of confidentiality.

6 Lead God's people in prayer and worship
Serve them with joy, build them up in faith

6.1 The clergy are called to leadership within the Church and the wider community.

6.2 They should develop this gift of leadership within their own ministry through prayer and training, being aware of their own natural leadership style.

6.3 The clergy should promote collaborative ministry across the whole range of church life and activity. It is important to recognize and affirm lay ministry that already exists and to encourage new ministries, both lay and ordained. The clergy should be ready to assist others in discerning and fulfilling their vocation and to acknowledge and respect the range of experience amongst the church membership.

6.4 The clergy should ensure that services are thoughtfully prepared, matching the need and culture of the parish or institution within the Anglican tradition.

6.5 Where appropriate, the clergy should involve others in leadership of worship, providing training and preparation as necessary to support them.

6.6 The clergy should be aware of the needs of their congregation and take any practical steps necessary to ensure that worship is truly inclusive and that no one is excluded through disability or disadvantage.

6.7 The clergy should encourage good ecumenical relationships.

6.8 Upon resignation or retirement, the clergy should immediately lay down their leadership and sever all professional relationships with those formerly under their pastoral cure. Any exception to this guideline should be formally negotiated with the bishop.

6.9 Having resigned or retired, the clergy should only minister in a former church, parish or institution if invited by the clergy with pastoral oversight or with their permission.

7 Call their hearers to repentance
In Christ's name absolve, and declare forgiveness of sins

7.1 The ministry of reconciliation, as an extension of Jesus' own ministry, lies at the heart of this vocation. It is to be exercised gently, patiently and undergirded by mutual trust.

7.2 There can be no disclosure of what is confessed to a priest. This principle holds even after the death of the penitent. The priest may not refer to what has been learnt in confession, even to the penitent, unless explicitly permitted. Some appropriate action of contrition and reparation may be required before absolution is given. A priest may withhold absolution.

7.3 Where abuse of children or vulnerable adults is admitted in the context of confession, the priest should urge the person to report his or her behaviour to the police or social services, and should also make this a condition of absolution, or withhold absolution until this evidence of repentance has been demonstrated.

7.4 If a penitent's behaviour gravely threatens his or her well-being or that of others, the priest, while advising action on the penitent's part, must still keep the confidence.

Note *An appeal to the tradition of the Church demonstrates this understanding of the 'seal of the confessional' and the relevant provision in the Canons of 1604 (Canon 113) was left unrepealed by the Canons of 1969, which superseded the earlier Canons in almost every other respect. Whether the civil courts will always respect this principle of absolute confidentiality remains uncertain.*

8   Will you accept the discipline of this Church, and give due respect to those in authority?

8.1 The clergy swear an oath of canonical obedience to the bishop. The clergy should participate fully in the life and work of deanery, archdeaconry, diocese and province, giving support and respect to those given the responsibility of leadership and oversight.

8.2 The clergy should know how canon and ecclesiastical law shape their exercise of office and ministry, and should respect such regulations as are put in place by the Church.

8.3 The authority of churchwardens and lay people elected or appointed to office in the local church is to be respected and affirmed.

9   Will you be diligent in prayer, in reading holy Scripture? Pray earnestly for his Holy Spirit

9.1 In exercising their ministry, the clergy respond to the call of our Lord Jesus Christ. The development of their discipleship is in the discipline of prayer, worship, Bible study and the discernment of the prompting of the Holy Spirit. The clergy should make sure that time and resources are available for their own personal and spiritual life and take responsibility for their own ongoing training and development.

9.2 Spiritual discernment can be facilitated by sharing the journey of faith with another person. A minister should have someone outside the work situation to whom to turn for help.

9.3 The clergy should participate fully in continuing ministerial education and in appraisal, knowing that accountability involves regular review personally and with others.

9.4 It is good practice for the clergy to meet regularly with a work consultant to review their ongoing ministry.

9.5 Time given to family life, friendship, recreation, renewal and personal health should be included in any review. This reflection will be the more useful if conducted both as part of a formal review and also in discussion with a spiritual director and work consultant.

10 Will you strive to fashion your own life and that of your household according to the way of Christ?

10.1 The clergy are called to a high standard of moral behaviour.

10.2 Those who are called to marriage should never forget that this is also a vocation. It should not be thought to be of secondary importance to their vocation to ministry. Similarly, those who are not married, including those with a vocation to celibacy, should take the necessary steps to nurture their lives, their friendships and their family relationships. All should guard themselves and their family against becoming victims of stress.

10.3 Good administration enables good pastoral care. Dealing with correspondence and enquiries with efficiency and courtesy is essential.

10.4 The keeping of parochial registers and records to a high standard is legally required as well as being part of pastoral care.

10.5 The clergy need to ensure that all their financial activities, whether personal or corporate, meet the highest ethical standards. There must be strict boundaries between church finance and personal moneys in order to avoid the possibility of suspicion or impropriety.

10.6 The clergy should never seek any personal advantage or gain by virtue of their clerical position.

10.7 The clergy should take care of their physical well-being. They should not undertake any professional duties when medically advised against it, nor under the influence of alcohol or drugs.

10.8 Blasphemous and offensive language is unacceptable.

11 Will you promote unity, peace and love among all Christian people?

11.1 The reputation of the Church in the community depends to a great extent on the example of its clergy, who should recognize their role as public representatives of the Church. Their lives should enhance and embody the communication of the gospel.

11.2 The clergy should ensure a reasonable level of availability and accessibility to the people of their parish or to those for whom they have a pastoral care. A prompt and gracious response to all requests for help demonstrates care.

11.3 The clergy have a particular role and calling as a catalyst of healing and as an agent of reconciliation for those in their charge.

11.4 The call of the clergy to be servants to the community should include their prophetic ministry to those in spiritual and moral danger.

12 Will you uphold them in their ministry?

12.1 'Care for the carers' is fundamental. The clergy need to be supported and the laity have a particular and significant role in the pastoral care of the clergy.

12.2 The officers of the parish, especially the churchwardens, should ensure that their clergy have:

- a safe environment in which to live and work;
- sufficient time off for rest, recreation and proper holidays;
- an annual opportunity to make a retreat of at least a week's duration;
- adequate administrative assistance;
- reimbursement in full of ministerial expenses (see the 'Parochial Expenses of the Clergy: A guide to their reimbursement' (Ministry Division, 2002));
- appropriate release for extra-parochial ministry;

- encouragement for ministry to the whole community and not just to the congregation.

12.3 The bishop takes responsibility for the welfare of the clergy when he receives the oath of canonical obedience. He shares this responsibility with suffragan and area bishops, archdeacons, and rural and area deans.

12.4 The clergy should be encouraged to develop opportunities for mutual support and pastoral care within chapters, cell groups, or other peer-groupings. All the clergy should also be encouraged to have a spiritual director, soul friend or confessor to support their spiritual life and help to develop their growth in self-understanding. If required, help should be given in finding such a person.

12.5 A directory or list of *Pastoral Care and Counselling* resources should be drawn up and made available in the diocese to the clergy and to their families, so that they can make their own arrangements to find help and support as they wish. Financial resources should be made available in the diocese to assist the clergy in paying for appropriate help if necessary. Confidentiality should be assured at every level. The boundaries between different persons involved in such care should therefore be recognized by all in the diocesan structures, not least where issues of financial assistance are involved. Advisers in pastoral care need to be especially careful to maintain these boundaries when making referrals or making reports to their diocesan colleagues.

12.6 The bishop or his trained representatives should undertake a regular review of each minister's work that should be clearly linked into the purposeful development of the individual's ministry, within the context of the needs of the Church.

12.7 Where some form of work consultancy for the clergy is available it should be offered by trained personnel whose work is monitored and reviewed by the bishop.

12.8 Clergy who are licensed under seal but not receiving a stipend should have a working agreement clearly setting out agreed boundaries of time and responsibility.

12.9 Each diocese has a duty to provide continuing ministerial education throughout a person's ministry. This should include adequate and suitable training in financial, administrative and managerial matters.

12.10 In dual ministries, where clergy have both a sector and a parochial responsibility, there should be a clear understanding between diocese, parish and the minister concerned about where the boundaries lie.

12.11 Support and advice on the practical, psychological and emotional issues involved should be readily available to clergy approaching retirement and to their families.

12.12 The bishop and those exercising pastoral care of the clergy should both by word and example actively encourage the clergy to adopt a healthy life-style. This should include adequate time for leisure, through taking days off and their full holiday entitlement, developing interests outside their main area of ministry, and maintaining a commitment to the care and development of themselves and their personal relationships. Helping the clergy understand and overcome unrealistic expectations within themselves and from the outside world needs to be a priority. Specific needs of married and of single clergy should be identified and addressed.

The clergy are privileged to be involved in the rites of passage, joys and sorrows, hopes and fears of the community. They should be particularly aware of both the opportunity this gives and the responsibility it carries. The laity of the Church are encouraged to do all in their power to ensure that they are as effective in their ministry as possible – even as the clergy must support them in theirs.

A theological reflection

Francis Bridger

In recent years, the Church of England has begun to debate the place of ethical guidelines in shaping the ministry of its clergy. This is a welcome development despite the fact that to some the thought of a code or set of guidelines is both risible and offensive. In their eyes it implies a lack of trust in ministerial integrity and an intrusion into sacred vocation. Even worse, it amounts to an unthinking acceptance of the cult of managerialism they fear has overtaken the ethos of the Church.

Consequently, the purpose of this reflection is twofold: (1) to address such concerns from a theological standpoint; and (2) to indicate the positive theological principles that underlie the guidelines contained in the present report. To be sure, there are sound pragmatic reasons why the Church must now face the question of a professional code for its clergy (and perhaps for its laity). But these form only one part of the argument. Alongside them must be set a number of theological justifications rooted in Scripture and moral theology.

Pragmatics, however, are important and it is worth rehearsing three reasons why this report has come into being:

- In the first place, it must be seen against the backdrop of General Synod's decision in 2000 to pass a new Clergy Discipline Measure. At the time of writing, that measure has still to be laid before Parliament; but once it has become law, it will be binding. Logically, discipline requires definition and this, in turn, points to the need for a code of practice or set of guidelines. The Convocations of Canterbury and York therefore established a working party to produce draft guidelines for consultation prior to further discussion at Synod. This report is the outcome.[1]

- Secondly, there is an urgent need for the Church to respond to current social pressures for greater regulation of professions – which has been achieved mainly by means of *self*-regulation. In the wake of a series of high-profile scandals relating to the medical profession and to social services (most notoriously of late, those of Harold Shipman and Victoria Climbié), a great deal more public concern now exists about the integrity and trustworthiness of previously respected professions. No longer are people willing automatically to give professionals the benefit of the doubt. They are subject to scrutiny and criticism in a way that was not true a generation ago. This presents a sizeable challenge to the Church; for it is simply not credible that the Church should expect to remain immune from such scrutiny.

Nor should it. Both tabloid newspaper headlines and more serious academic studies bear witness to the dark side of the Church's life, which cannot be denied. On one hand, there are the perennial stories of vicars involved in sexual shenanigans with parishioners, while on the other, investigation of child abuse by clergy demonstrates that the Church must take its share of blame for a phenomenon that has been all too readily denied by society until recent years.[2] Other studies published in the United States also bear witness to the ever-present dangers of sexual misconduct that are a constant threat to godly ministry.[3] Consequently, no one should underestimate the risks inherent in ministerial – especially pastoral – practice. Compared to some other professions, clergy may still enjoy a high level of trust but this does not preclude the need for accountability and transparency.[4]

- Thirdly, there is the 'nightmare scenario' that all clergy dread: the parishioner who accuses his or her minister of misconduct – often sexual but sometimes taking the form of a different kind of abuse.[5] This is the situation that every pastor fears, irrespective of its veracity. The mere accusation by itself is enough to ruin a minister's credibility and standing. It does not have to be true in order to destroy: the slightest of rumours immediately undermines trust and exposes a clergyman or woman to the charge of hypocrisy. No matter that such rumours might be without foundation and maliciously intended.

In such circumstances, the Clergy Discipline Procedures and the guidelines contained in the present report are designed to protect three parties: the accused, the accuser and the Church. It is important to mention the last of these because it can easily be forgotten that professional ethics are not simply a matter for individuals. While they undoubtedly exist to guide and protect individuals they also serve to safeguard the profession. They are an expression of mutual accountability and responsibility. When one clergyman or woman acts unprofessionally, he or she threatens to bring the Church as a whole into disrepute – witness the ripple effect of scandals. As Eric Mount has commented: 'Moral responsibility includes being responsible people within institutions.'[6] Or in Paul's words, 'we are members of one another' (Ephesians 4.25).[7]

The Clergy Discipline Measure provides a mechanism whereby justice can be done and can be seen to be done (not least for the accused); the guidelines produced by the Convocations' Working Party supply a framework for behaviour that would make less likely the possibility of a nightmare scenario arising in the first place. For, in many instances, it is not intentional actions that arouse suspicion and give rise to accusations. Rather, it is simple naivety, such as inappropriately affectionate touching or hugging that might be meant as gestures of affirmation but are interpreted as signs of sexual interest. The guidelines offer a framework for avoiding such situations.

Pragmatic reasons in themselves, though, are not enough. They are a necessary but not sufficient justification for the cultural change required within the Church if it is to be prepared for the kind of scrutiny presupposed by contemporary society. It is here that a *theology of professional responsibility* becomes central. And it is to this that we must now turn.

The starting point for any discussion of professionalism must be the principle of *vocation*. It is axiomatic that ordained ministry is first and foremost a calling that originates within the purposes of God. The sense that they are engaged in a vocation rather than a career is fundamental to the clergy's identity and self-understanding. Yet this is sometimes used as a kind of knock-down argument against the introduction of guidelines or a professional code of practice on the grounds that 'to "professionalize" pastoral ministry is to reduce it to tasks and to ignore its spiritual, transcendent dimension'.[8] Against this, as a number of writers note, it needs to be remembered that:

(a)   historically, the notion of profession has its roots in a religious connection between profession and vocation;[9]

(b)   the idea of *professio* (from which the term 'profession' derives) carries with it the meaning of 'standing for something' or 'value laden';

(c)   the identification of professionalism with technocratic expertise is a modern development which has served unduly and untheologically to narrow the concept; and

(d)   by means of a theology of vocation, it becomes possible to reinvest the idea of profession with a transcendent, moral dimension, thereby drawing the sting of the critic in one respect at least.

In Richard Gula's words, 'Aligning "having a vocation" with "being a professional" . . . affirms all that we do in ministry is a response to the presence of God in and through the community calling us to act on its behalf as signs and agents of God's love.'[10]

In the light of this, the criticism that a code of practice amounts to a concession to managerialism must be seen as misplaced. The establishment of guidelines that indicate what it means to act in a manner consistent with a calling to ministry can be seen as an attempt to work out in concrete terms the practice of vocation in a contemporary setting. 'Profession', in a clergy context, must therefore be seen as possessing a dual meaning: on one hand to describe the sociological reality of a group of people who operate according to conventions and practices developed by the group for functional purposes; and on the other, as an indication that this group stands for – professes – a set of transcendent values and principles which derive from a theology of vocation. Both senses of the term 'profession' must be kept in mind.

From the principle of vocation follows the question: a vocation to what? The most obvious answer is 'to serve'. But to serve whom? Theologically, service is firstly towards God and only secondly towards human beings. Moreover, such service is only possible through relationship. This, in turn, requires the teasing out of a cluster of concepts that shape the notions of relationship and relationality. And at the centre of this cluster lies the idea of covenant.

Covenant

It is arguable that the doctrine of covenant represents the wellspring from which a theology of professional responsibility flows. Its significance can be demonstrated by contrasting it with the concept which governs secular models of professional relationship, namely that of contract. As Richard Gula has pointed out, the two are close cousins but there are crucial differences. Contracts define the specific nature of the relationship and the precise rights and duties that follow from it. Neither party can expect the other to go beyond the specified contractual duties and each has the liberty to refuse requests to do so. Indeed, the expectation is that such requests will not be made or granted except in extremis. 'The contract model acknowledges human limitations of the contracting parties since it clearly distinguishes rights and duties. It circumscribes the kind and amount of service being sought and offered.'[11] By contrast, the biblical model of covenant – exemplified most powerfully by the covenant relationship between God and his people – is based upon grace. The covenant partners are bound together not by a set of legal requirements but by the relational nexus of gracious initiative followed by thankful response. Covenant goes further than the carefully defined obligations contained within a contract to the need for further actions that might be required by love. 'When we act according to a covenant, we look beyond the minimum . . . Partners in a covenant are willing to go the extra mile to make things work out.'[12]

It is this graciousness – the readiness 'to make room for the gratuitous, not just the gratuities'[13] – that distinguishes covenant from contract and gives ministry its distinctive quality. Rooted in the covenant love of God, the covenantal ministry of clergy mirrors that of Christ himself who gave himself freely for the sake of the world and 'who, though he was in the form of God, did not regard equality with God as something to be exploited but emptied himself, taking the form of a slave' (Philippians 2.6-7). The covenant model is, in the end, Christological or it is nothing.

16

The implication of this is that those who are called to ordained ministry must act out of a covenantal rather than a contractual motivation and mindset. They must be 'willing to go the extra mile' which means that they must be prepared to allow their ministry to be shaped by the needs of others rather than their own preconceptions of autonomy. But how might this be worked out? This leads us to two further principles: agape and virtue.

Agape

In a recent discussion of agape and pastoral care, Simon Robinson notes that agape and covenant are intimately connected in a number of ways: firstly, both are based upon gift, for just as covenant is gracious so agape is a matter of gift-love. In pastoral terms, agape 'is not based upon any contractual terms' but is 'a way of knowing the other, the ground of care for the other'.[14] Pastoral relationships are thus governed by agape. Secondly, agape involves faithfulness and constancy. The minister remains true to the other person whatever he or she has done, since 'agape promises to be there whatever the response from the other.'[15] Thirdly, agape allows for a measure of relational open-endedness rather than placing rigid limitations on the growth of a pastoral relationship. This is not to deny the importance of boundaries; yet, at the same time, it 'nourishes rather than limits relationships' and 'is always searching for the good of the other . . . is always open to the possibilities of the other'.[16] From this it can be seen that agapeic love is not conditioned by the attraction or achievement of the other but 'loves the other simply because they are the other'. It is 'a love which does not base itself on the action of the other, a disinterested love which is not based in a partial way on the other'.[17]

How might this theology be applied? Secular pastoral counselling (building on work in bioethics) has developed five operational principles as the basis for its professional codes. If we invest them with the theological concept of agape, it becomes possible to construe them as a principled framework for ethical practice in ordained ministry:

1. the promotion of autonomy for the counsellee;
2. the duty of the counsellor to act for the positive good of the counsellee (the principle of beneficence);
3. the responsibility of the counsellor to do no harm (the principle of non-maleficence);
4. the obligation to act justly in the counsellee's best interests (the principle of justice);
5. the counsellor's commitment to trustworthiness (the principle of fidelity).

While the term 'agape' does not appear, from a theological perspective it can be discerned as the theological meta-principle lying behind all five. And if we were to substitute the terms 'parishioner' for 'counsellee' and 'minister' for 'counsellor', the transference to a set of principles for Christian ministry becomes clear.

What is equally clear, however, is that while one purpose of this framework is to protect the counsellor/minister, its fundamental emphasis is on the needs of the client/parishioner. In Robinson's language, the principles are directed towards the well-being of the Other. The rights of the helper are secondary to the good of the one who seeks help. This in turn means that those of us who are called upon to offer ministerial care must be prepared to allow our independence to be qualified as we test our ministry against the demands of professional guidelines informed by agape. The body of this report gives substance to this.

Nowhere is the importance of agapeic principles more clearly seen than in the issue of power. Within the relationship between clergy and parishioners, it is crucial to appreciate that power is used asymmetrically. That is to say, the clergyman or woman is more powerful than the person seeking help. Although self-evident upon reflection, this is a fact which is all too easily overlooked. At its worst, the wielding of asymmetrical power leads to abuse, sexual and otherwise. The vicar who uses her power to coerce, manipulate or bully an individual into agreement is every bit as abusive – albeit in a different way – as the vicar who uses his status to satisfy his sexual desires. Both are exercising power to achieve their own ends in contravention of the principles above.

Rollo May has developed a typology of power that enables us to identify what kind of power is being used at any given time.[18] According to May, power can be discerned under five headings:

- *exploitative* power that dominates by force and coercion;
- *manipulative* power that controls by more subtle and covert psychological means;
- *competitive* power that is ambiguous since it can be used constructively where parties are relatively equal but is destructive where they are unequal (as in most pastoral relationships);
- *nutritive* power that sustains and empowers;
- *integrative* power that takes the freedom of others seriously and seeks to harness the other person's (potential) strengths.

This typology offers a grid by which particular ministerial exercises of power can be assessed. The first two types clearly fall outside a covenantal/agapeic understanding of ministry since they are not concerned with the needs or good of the other person at all. The third is questionable, though capable of constructive use in some situations.

The fourth and fifth accord well with a theology of covenant and agape because they arise out of a desire to further the best interests of the other.

From a ministerial perspective, therefore, 'the moral challenge is to see that in our interaction with others, the right use of power moves away from dominating others through exploitation and manipulation, and that it moves toward liberating others through nutrient and integrative acts of power'.[19] When seeking to achieve our objectives – whether with a group of people or in a one-to-one relationship – we must ask ourselves what kind of power we are seeking to exercise and for whose benefit. If the answer to either of these questions points to ourselves, we need to return to the five agapeic principles.

In summary, therefore, it can be seen that if ministry is to be based on a concept of covenantal responsibility from which agapeic practice flows, this will require a more substantive set of professional criteria than a simple appeal to the beatitudes or any other general idea. As the example of power shows, a more complex approach is needed if we are to grasp both the theological nature of ministerial relationships and the implications for practice that must follow.

Virtue

Ethical behaviour, however, is not just a matter of adherence to rules or principles. The revival of 'virtue ethics' among moral philosophers and theologians in recent years reminds us that the character of the professional is as important as the code to which he or she adheres.[20] The ethics of conduct must be shaped by the ethics of character and the ethics of integrity.

What does this mean? According to William Willimon, character can be defined as the 'basic moral orientation that gives unity, definition and direction to our lives by forming our habits into meaningful and predictable patterns that have been determined by our dominant convictions'.[21] What we do is governed by who we are. As Stanley Hauerwas notes, each of us makes moral choices arising out of 'the dispositions, experience, traditions, heritage and virtues that he or she has cultivated'.[22]

From this, two points stand out: firstly, the Christian minister must *deliberately* cultivate Christian character and virtues and not leave them to chance. In Pauline language, he or she must seek the fruits of the Spirit: love, joy, peace, patience, kindness, generosity, faithfulness, gentleness, self-control (Galatians 5.22-23). When we ask what this might entail in terms of professional ethics, Karen Lebacqz argues for two central virtues: trustworthiness and prudence. The former is a matter of integrity or honour so that the minister is recognized as a 'trustworthy trustee'. The latter has to do with wise judgement or discernment. The combination of both is necessary for the minister to develop an instinct for doing the right.

Secondly, we are brought back to the idea of 'habits of the heart' suggested (*inter alia*) by Willimon. Because these arise out of the kind of people we are, our theological convictions and spiritual practices are crucial to professional life. We are formed by the beliefs we hold and ways in which we relate to God. Doctrine, ethics and spirituality go hand in hand 'to the point of behaving ethically most of the time as though by instinct.'[23] The report's discussion of the Ordinal recognizes this and reminds us that the sustenance of virtue cannot be left to chance. The spiritual life of the minister is crucial.

But it has to be remembered that behind all Christian versions of virtue ethics stands grace. The power to be and do right flows from the free self-giving of God in Christ. It is through the indwelling Holy Spirit that we are enabled to grow in character and virtue. We become trustworthy trustees and are sustained in ministry by the activity of God in us. Ministerial codes or guidelines may set the boundaries but only by grace can we live them out. In Richard Gula's words, 'If we are to minister in the spirit of Jesus and continue in our own time his mission of proclaiming the reign of God, then we must be free enough in ourselves to accept God's offer of love and so be free for others to enable them to let go of whatever keeps them from accepting divine love as well.'[24]

Conclusion

This has necessarily been but a brief sketch of the central issues underlying the present report: a mapping of the terrain rather than an exhaustive journey through it. We have seen how the Church can no longer stand back from addressing the issue of what it means to act professionally in today's social climate. Moreover, we have noted that to develop a culture of professional ethics will require not just a set of guidelines for practice but the cultivation of virtuous character based on theology, morality and spirituality. Above all, we are reminded that the foundational value for all Christian ethics is the uniquely Christian gift of agape. Without this we are but clanging cymbals, professional or otherwise.

Francis Bridger
Trinity College, Bristol
Epiphany 2002

Notes

1. For examples of codes from other denominations, see Joe E. Trull and James E. Carter, *Ministerial Ethics*, Broadman & Holman, 1993, pp. 220–56. Richard M. Gula in his *Ethics in Pastoral Ministry* (New York: Paulist Press, 1996, pp. 142–153) sets out a proposed code which is valuable for its theological rationale as well as its specific proposals.

2. See Steve Gillhooley, *The Pyjama Parade*, Edinburgh: Lomond Publishers, 2000.

3. See, for example, Karen Lebacqz and Ronald G. Barton, *Sex in the Parish*, Louisville: Westminster/ John Knox Press, 1991; Marie Fortune, *Is Nothing Sacred? When Sex Invades the Pastoral Relationship*, San Francisco: Harper & Row, 1989.

4. On the debate as to how far the clergy should be understood as professionals and therefore to what extent the models employed by 'the professions' are relevant, see Karen Lebacqz and Joseph D. Driskill, *Ethics and Spiritual Care*, Nashville: Abingdon Press 2000, ch. 2. Also, Eric Mount Jr, Professional Ethics in Context, Louisville: Westminster/John Knox Press, 1990, chs 2 and 3.

5. A recent term that has entered discussion is 'spiritual abuse'. On its meaning and validity see Lebacqz and Driskill, *Ethics and Spiritual Care*, ch. 6.

6. Eric Mount Jr, *Professional Ethics in Context: Institutions, Images and Empathy*, Louisville: Westminster/John Knox Press, 1990, p. 45.

7. Significantly, Paul uses the language of mutual interdependence as justification for the code of community ethics he goes on to outline in this passage (verses 26f.).

8. Gula, *Ethics in Pastoral Ministry*, p. 11.

9. Thus Darrell Reeck notes that, 'Judaeo-Christian culture from Biblical times through the Reformation imbued the concept of *profession* with the moral concept of service grounded in a religious vision of God working together with people for the improvement of all creation. The doctrine of the *vocation* or *calling* became the religious and moral theme that most illuminated the meaning of the professions and professional work.' Reeck, *Ethics for the Professions: A Christian Perspective*, Minneapolis: Augsburg, 1982, p. 33 quoted in Trull and Carter, *Ministerial Ethics*, p. 25.

10. Gula, *Ethics in Pastoral Ministry*, p. 14.

11. Gula, *Ethics in Pastoral Ministry*, p. 15.

12. Gula, *Ethics in Pastoral Ministry*, p. 15.

13. Gula, *Ethics in Pastoral Ministry*, p. 15.

14. Simon J. Robinson, *Agape, Moral Meaning and Pastoral Counselling*, Cardiff: Aureus Publishing, 2001, pp. 44, 43. For a recent discussion of agape as the basis for a comprehensive Christian ethic, see Stanley J. Grenz, *The Moral Quest: Foundations of Christian Ethics*, Leicester: Apollos, 1997, ch. 8.

15. Robinson, *Agape*, p. 45.

16. Robinson, *Agape*, p. 45.

17. Robinson, *Agape*, p. 44.

18. Rollo May, *Power and Innocence*, New York: W. W. Norton & Co., 1972, ch. 5. See also, Karen Lebacqz, *Professional Ethics: Power and Paradox*, Nashville: Abingdon Press, 1985.

19. Gula, *Ethics in Pastoral Ministry*, p. 86.

20. On the importance of virtue ethics, see Joseph J. Kotva, *The Christian Case for Virtue Ethics*, Washington DC: Georgetown University Press, 1996.

21. Quoted in Trull and Carter, *Ministerial Ethics*, p. 47.

22. Trull and Carter, *Ministerial Ethics*, p. 47.

23. Walter E. Wiest and Elwyn A. Smith, *Ethics in Ministry: A Guide for the Professional*, Minneapolis: Fortress Press, 1990, p. 182.

24. Gula, *Ethics in Pastoral Ministry*, p. 29.